P9-DFN-753

GERMAN COOKING

Norma MacMillan

Picture credits
Paul Bussell: 45.
Alan Duns: 5, 17, 21, 33, 53.
Paul Kemp: 37.
Don Last: 9.
Roger Phillips: 13, 41, 57, 61.
Iain Reid: 33.
Heini Schneebeli: 25, 29, 49.

Edited by Isabel Moore

Produced by

Marshall Cavendish Books Limited
58 Old Compton Street
London W1V 5PA

© Marshall Cavendish Limited 1981

First printing 1981

Printed in Singapore

CONTENTS

SOUPS & STARTERS

Linsensuppe

(Lentil and vegetable soup)

---

2 cups lentils, soaked overnight and drained
5 pints boiling water
$\frac{1}{2}$ lb piece of lean bacon
1 leek, chopped
2 large carrots, peeled and chopped
2 celery stalks, chopped
2 tablespoons oil
2 medium onions, finely chopped
2 tablespoons flour
$1\frac{1}{2}$ tablespoons cider vinegar
$\frac{1}{2}$ lb garlic sausage, diced

1. Put the lentils in a saucepan with the boiling water, bacon, vegetables and salt. Bring back to a boil, then simmer for 45 minutes.

2. Meanwhile, heat the oil in a skillet. Add the onions and fry until softened. Sprinkle over the flour and stir in well. Cook for a further 3 minutes or until golden brown.

3. Remove the skillet from the heat and stir in about 1 cup of the soup until the mixture is thick and creamy. Stir in the vinegar, then add this mixture to the remaining soup. Stir well. Cover and simmer for 1 hour or until the lentils are tender.

4. Remove the bacon and cut it into dice. Return the bacon dice to the soup with the sausage, and salt and pepper to taste. Simmer for 5 minutes to heat the sausage.

Serves 6

Biersuppe mit Schneebergen

(Beer soup with floating islands)

---

3 cups brown beer
¼ cup sugar
grated rind of 1 lemon
2 whole cloves
⅛ teaspoon ground cinnamon
4 teaspoons cornstarch
2 eggs, separated
2 teaspoons confectioners' sugar

1. Preheat the oven to 425°. Put the beer, sugar, a pinch of salt, lemon rind, and spices in a flameproof casserole and bring slowly to a boil, stirring to dissolve the sugar. Dissolve the cornstarch in a little of the beer, then add to the rest of the beer in the casserole. Simmer, stirring, for 3 minutes.

2. Remove the casserole from the heat and stir in the egg yolks. Beat the egg whites until stiff. Add the confectioners' sugar and beat for a further 1 minute. Place spoonsful of the egg white mixture on top of the beer soup.

3. Put the soup into the oven and cook for about 5 minutes or until the 'meringues' are lightly browned.

Serves 4

Markklosschensuppe

(Marrow dumpling soup)

---

5 oz fresh beef marrow
1 egg, separated
1 cup fresh breadcrumbs
¾ cup chopped parsley
pinch of grated nutmeg
1 teaspoon salt
1 quart beef stock or consommé

1. Crush the marrow and mix it with the egg yolk, bread-crumbs, parsley, nutmeg, and salt. Beat the egg white until stiff and fold into the mixture. Leave to stand for about 10 minutes.

2. Bring the stock or consommé to a boil in a saucepan. Form the marrow mixture into small dumplings using a teaspoon (dip it each time into hot water). Drop them into the stock or consommé and simmer until tender.

Serves 4

Bauernsuppe

(*Peasant soup*)

---

4 tablespoons butter
2 lb chuck steak, cut into small cubes
2 onions, chopped
$\frac{1}{4}$ cup flour
1 garlic clove, crushed
1 teaspoon paprika
$5\frac{1}{2}$ pints beef stock
1 bouquet garni
2 large potatoes, peeled and diced
$1\frac{1}{2}$ teaspoons chopped fresh dill
$\frac{1}{2}$ cup grated cheese

1. Melt the butter in a Dutch oven. Add the steak cubes and brown on all sides. Add the onions and fry until softened. Stir in the flour, garlic, paprika, and salt and pepper to taste and cook gently for 5 minutes.

2. Gradually stir in the stock and bring to a boil. Add the bouquet garni. Cover and simmer for 1 hour, stirring occasionally.

3. Add the potatoes and stir well. Cover again and continue simmering for 45 minutes.

4. Discard the bouquet garni. Ladle the soup into individual bowls and sprinkle with the dill and cheese. Serve hot.

Serves 6

Bean Soup with Apples

1 lb green beans
¾ lb potatoes, peeled and diced
2 quarts beef stock
1 bunch of summer savory
1 lb tart apples, peeled, cored, and sliced
¼ lb slab bacon, diced
1 onion, finely chopped
4 teaspoons flour
2 teaspoons vinegar
sugar

1. Remove the strings from the beans, if necessary, then cut them diagonally into small pieces. Put the beans in a saucepan with the potatoes and stock. Bring to a boil, then simmer for 45 minutes.

2. Add the summer savory and continue simmering for 5 minutes. Stir in the apples and simmer for a further 10 minutes.

3. Meanwhile, fry the bacon and onion together in a skillet until they are lightly browned. Sprinkle over the flour and stir in well. Cook for 1 minute, then gradually stir in about ½ cup of the stock from the saucepan.

4. Stir the bacon mixture into the soup in the saucepan. Add the vinegar with salt and sugar to taste. Simmer, stirring, until the soup has thickened, then serve.

Serves 6–8

Sahneheringe

(Herring salad)

---

8 large salted herring fillets, soaked in cold water for 4 hours
2 cups sour cream
1 large dill pickle, chopped
2 firm tart apples, cored and chopped
2 onions, chopped
4 teaspoons chopped chives
Marinade
3 tablespoons vinegar
3 tablespoons water
3 tablespoons sugar

1. Drain the herring fillets and pat dry with paper towels.

2. Mix together the marinade ingredients in a shallow dish. Add the herring fillets and turn to coat with the marinade. Leave to marinate for a few hours, turning occasionally.

3. Drain the herring fillets and arrange them on a serving plate. Pour the sour cream over them, then sprinkle the pickle, apples, onions, and chives over the top. Serve with baked potatoes and beer.

Serves 6–8

NOTE: In Germany, this dish is usually made with salted herring fillets, which are not always available in the U.S. If you prefer to make the recipe with pickled herrings fillets, remember to omit the marinade ingredients and step 2 of the recipe.

Wurstsalat

(Sausage salad)

---

1 lb mixed cooked German wurst, sliced
1 green (bell) pepper, cored, seeded, and sliced
1 sweet red pepper, cored, seeded, and sliced
1 onion, thinly sliced into rings
2 small dill pickles, halved
Dressing
5 tablespoons salad oil
2 tablespoons vinegar
½ teaspoon Dijon mustard

1. Arrange the wurst and peppers on a serving plate. Scatter over the onion rings and garnish with the pickle halves.

2. Mix together the ingredients for the dressing and pour over the salad. Chill for 30 minutes before serving.

Serves 4

FISH

Gefullter Maifisch

(Stuffed Garfish)

---

4 garfish or mackerel, cleaned
2 tablespoons flour
8 tablespoons (1 stick) butter
Stuffing
½ cup chopped cooked ham
4 tomatoes
4 slices of white bread, crusts removed
1 parsley sprig
½ cup milk

1. Preheat the oven to 325°. Rub the insides of the fish with salt.

2. To make the stuffing, grind together the ham, tomatoes, bread, and parsley, or purée in a food processor. Add salt to taste and the milk and mix well. Loosely stuff the fish with this mixture and sew up the opening.

3. Coat the fish with the flour. Melt the butter in a shallow flameproof casserole. Add the fish and brown on all sides. Transfer the casserole to the oven and cook for 30 minutes.

4. Serve hot with potato salad.

Serves 4

Perch Fillets
with Mustard Butter

2 lb perch fillets, skinned
juice of 1 lemon
12 tablespoons (1½ sticks) butter
1 onion, finely chopped
1 teaspoon canned green peppercorns, crushed
1 tablespoon strong mustard
2 tablespoons whipping cream
chopped parsley to garnish

1. Place the perch fillets on a plate and sprinkle with the lemon juice. Leave to soak for 10 minutes.

2. Pat the fish dry with paper towels, then season them with salt and pepper to taste. Melt 4 tablespoons of the butter in a skillet. Add the fish and fry for 5 minutes on each side or until cooked. Remove the fish from the pan and keep hot on a warmed serving platter.

3. Wipe out the skillet with the paper towels, then melt the rest of the butter in it. Add the onion and fry until softened. Stir in the peppercorns and mustard and cook for a further 2 minutes. Stir in the cream and pour this sauce over the fish. Sprinkle with chopped parsley and serve.

Serves 6

Katerfrühstück

(Pickled flounder)

1½ lb flounder fillets
juice of 1 lemon
4 tablespoons butter
3 medium onions, sliced
2 large tomatoes, skinned, seeded, and chopped
2 tablespoons tomato paste
1 tablespoon white wine vinegar
½ teaspoon dried dill
3 dill pickles, thinly sliced

1. Put the fish fillets on a plate and sprinkle with the lemon juice and salt and pepper to taste. Leave to soak for 15 minutes. Preheat the oven to 375°.

2. Meanwhile, melt 2 tablespoons of the butter in a skillet. Add the onions and tomatoes and cook until the onions are softened. Remove the skillet from the heat.

3. Mix together the tomato paste, vinegar and dill in a small bowl.

4. Drain the fish fillets and arrange them, in one layer, in a greased shallow baking dish. Spread the vinegar mixture over the fish, then pour over the onion mixture. Cover with the slices of dill pickle. Cut the remaining butter into small pieces and dot these on top.

5. Bake for 15–20 minutes or until the fish flakes easily when tested with a fork. Serve hot.

Serves 6

MEAT

Gaisburger Marsch

(Beef stew with dumplings)

---

4 tablespoons butter
1½ lb beef chuck, cubed
2 cups beef stock
1 teaspoon vinegar
4 potatoes, peeled and cubed
3 tablespoons oil
2 large onions, thinly sliced into rings
Dumplings
2 cups flour
1 teaspoon salt
2 eggs, beaten
¾ cup milk

1. Melt the butter in a Dutch oven. Add the beef cubes and brown on all sides. Stir in the stock, vinegar, and salt and pepper and bring to a boil. Cover and simmer for 30 minutes. Add the potatoes and simmer for 1 hour or until the beef is tender.

2. To make the dumplings, sift the flour and salt into a bowl. Beat in the eggs, then the milk. 'Rest' for 10 minutes.

3. Drop ½ teaspoonsful of the batter, a few at a time, into a saucepan of boiling water and cook for 4 minutes or until soft when pressed against the side of the pan. Drain on paper towels. Stir the dumplings into the stew and cook for 10 minutes.

4. Heat the oil in a skillet. Add the onions and fry until golden. Drain on paper towels. Serve the stew topped with the onions.

Serves 4–6

Sauerbraten

(Marinated sweet and sour beef)

---

1 × 3½ lb beef top round roast
¼ cup cooking oil
2 medium onions, sliced
3 carrots, peeled and quartered lengthwise
2 tablespoons butter
¼ cup flour
¼ lb lebkuchen, crumbled
½ cup slivered almonds
Marinade
2½ cups water
1¼ cups red wine vinegar
1¼ cups red wine
4 garlic cloves, halved
1 tablespoon mustard seed
1 tablespoon black peppercorns, crushed

1. Put the beef in a plastic bag and add all the marinade ingredients. Close and refrigerate for 3 days. Remove the beef and pat dry with paper towels. Strain the marinade and reserve.

2. Heat the oil in a Dutch oven. Add the beef and brown on all sides. Add the onions, carrots, and 2½ cups of the marinade. Bring to a boil, then cover and simmer for 2½ hours.

3. Transfer the beef and vegetables to a platter, slice and keep hot. Strain the cooking juices and measure them. If they do not make 2½ cups, add some of the remaining marinade.

4. Melt the butter in a pan. Stir in the flour for 2 minutes. Gradually stir in the cooking juices and bring to a boil. Simmer until thickened. Stir in the lebkuchen and almonds. Cover and simmer gently for 10 minutes. Serve with the meat.

Serves 6

Boiled Beef
with Lemon Sauce

---

1 × 4 lb beef bottom round roast
4 tablespoons oil
6 black peppercorns
thinly paired rind of 1 small lemon
2 pints chicken stock
Sauce
6 tablespoons butter
2 tablespoons flour
3 tablespoons lemon juice
¼ lb button mushrooms, quartered
1 egg yolk
2 tablespoons sour cream

1. Rub the beef all over with salt. Heat the oil in a Dutch oven. Add the beef and brown on all sides. Add the peppercorns, lemon rind, and stock. Bring to a boil, then cover and cook gently for 2½ hours or until the beef is very tender. Remove the beef from the pot and keep hot. Strain the cooking liquid into a measuring jug. Skim off the fat and reserve 2 cups of the liquid.

2. Melt 2 tablespoons of the butter in a saucepan. Stir in the flour and cook for 1 minute. Gradually stir in the reserved liquid. Bring to a boil, and simmer until thick. Stir in the lemon juice and salt and pepper. Cook gently for 5 minutes.

3. Melt the remaining butter in a skillet. Add the mushrooms and cook for 3 minutes, then stir into the sauce.

4. Beat the egg yolk and sour cream together. Add a little hot sauce, then stir into the rest in the pan. Cook gently until thick. Slice the beef and arrange on a platter. Pour over the sauce.

Serves 8

Rouladen

(Stuffed beef rolls)

---

6 slices of beef rump, about 6 × 8 inches
6 teaspoons mustard
1 tablespoon capers
1 tablespoon seedless white raisins
1 large onion, finely chopped
5 tablespoons butter
4 carrots, peeled and finely chopped
3 tomatoes, skinned, seeded, and chopped
1 teaspoon sugar
1¾ cups red wine
1 tablespoon flour

1. Beat the beef slices with a rolling pin until very thin. Lay them out flat and spread over 1 teaspoon of mustard. Sprinkle with the capers, raisins and onion, then roll up and tie with thread.

2. Melt 4 tablespoons of the butter in a Dutch oven. Add the beef rolls and brown on all sides. Remove them from the pot. Add the remaining onion and carrots and fry until softened. Stir in the tomatoes, and sugar, and cook for 5 minutes.

3. Stir in the wine and bring to a boil. Return the beef rolls, cover and simmer for 1 hour. Remove from the pot.

4. Strain the cooking liquid into a saucepan. Bring to a boil and boil for 15 minutes or until reduced by about one-third.

5. Mix the remaining butter with the flour to make a smooth paste. Add a little of the cooking liquid, then stir into the remaining liquid in the pan. Simmer, stirring, until smooth.

6. Return the beef rolls to the sauce and reheat for 5 minutes.

Serves 6

Pichelsteiner

(Meat and vegetable casserole)

---

4 tablespoons oil
½ lb boneless lamb, cut into 1 inch cubes
½ lb boneless pork, cut into 1 inch cubes
½ lb beef chuck, cut into ½ inch cubes
½ lb boneless veal, cut into ½ inch cubes
2 large carrots, peeled and sliced
½ small head of cabbage, cored and shredded
¼ lb green beans, sliced
4 celery stalks, sliced
1 medium turnip, peeled and chopped
2 leeks, white parts only, sliced
1 cup shelled fresh peas
1 large onion, chopped
2 large potatoes, peeled and diced
¼ lb beef marrow, chopped
2 cups beef stock

1. Heat the oil in a skillet. Add the lamb cubes and brown on all sides. Remove from the pan. Brown the remaining meats in the same way. Mix together all the vegetables.

2. Cover the bottom of a large Dutch oven with the beef marrow. Make alternate layers of the meats and vegetable mixture on top, sprinkling each layer with salt and pepper. Pour in the stock. Cover the pot and simmer for 2 hours or until all the meats are tender. Serve hot.

Serves 4–6

Königsberger Klopse

(Meatballs in piquant sauce)

$\frac{1}{2}$ *lb boneless pork, cubed*
$\frac{1}{2}$ *lb beef chuck, cubed*
$\frac{1}{4}$ *lb slab bacon, cubed*
2 onions, quartered
2 slices of white bread
1 teaspoon chopped anchovy fillets
4 eggs
Sauce
4 tablespoons butter
4 teaspoons flour
$\frac{1}{4}$ *cup cream*
2 egg yolks
2 teaspoons vinegar
1 teaspoon sugar
2 teaspoons capers

1. Grind together the meats, onions, and bread, or use a food processor. Add the anchovies, eggs, and salt and pepper and mix together. Form the mixture into large meatballs.

2. Drop the meatballs into boiling salted water and simmer for 20 minutes or until just tender. Remove the meatballs with a slotted spoon and keep hot. Reserve 2 cups of the liquid.

3. Melt the butter in the clean saucepan. Stir in the flour and cook for 2 minutes. Gradually stir in the reserved cooking liquid. Bring to a boil, stirring, and simmer until thickened.

4. Beat the cream and egg yolks together. Add a little hot sauce, then stir into the rest of the sauce in the pan. Cook gently, stirring, until very thick. Stir in the vinegar, sugar, capers, and salt and pepper. Add the meatballs and reheat gently.

Serves 4

Berliner Eintopf

(Berlin stew)

---

3 tablespoons butter
1 large onion, chopped
3 potatoes, peeled and diced
$\frac{1}{2}$ lb green beans, chopped
2 carrots, peeled and diced
$\frac{1}{2}$ head of cabbage, cored and cut into 4 pieces
2 cups beef stock
1 tablespoon tomato catsup
1 teaspoon mustard
$\frac{1}{4}$ cup fresh breadcrumbs
$1\frac{1}{2}$ lb cooked beef, veal or pork, cut into thin strips or diced
chopped parsley to garnish

1. Melt the butter in a Dutch oven. Add the onion and fry until softened. Stir in the potatoes, beans, carrots, and cabbage and fry for a further 2 minutes.

2. Add the stock, catsup, mustard, and salt and pepper to taste and stir well. Cover and cook gently for 40 minutes.

3. Stir in the breadcrumbs and meat and cook for a further 5 minutes or until the stew is thick and the meat is heated through. Serve hot, sprinkled with parsley.

Serves 4

Hoppelpoppel

(Hash)

---

4 tablespoons lard or butter
1 cup diced leftover roast beef or pork
1 cup diced cooked ham
1 cup diced sausages or frankfurters
1 lb potatoes, cooked in their skins, cooled and chopped
2 onions, finely chopped
4 eggs, beaten
chopped parsley to garnish

1. Melt the lard or butter in a large skillet. Add the meats and potatoes and fry until all are lightly browned and piping hot. Stir in the onions, eggs, and salt and pepper to taste and continue cooking, stirring constantly, until the eggs are lightly scrambled.

2. Serve immediately, sprinkled with parsley.

Serves 4

Eisbein auf Sauerkraut

(Pickled pork with sauerkraut)

---

1 onion
1 × 4 lb smoked pork picnic roast
5 coriander seeds
5 black peppercorns, coarsely crushed
4 teaspoons salt
2 lb canned sauerkraut, drained and roughly chopped
4 tablespoons pork drippings
2 onions, finely chopped
1¼ cups dry white wine
1 potato, peeled and grated
2 teaspoons sugar

1. Cut the unpeeled onion in half. Heat a skillet and brown the cut surfaces of the onion (this gives the gravy a better color).

2. Put the pork in a Dutch oven and add the onion, coriander seeds, peppercorns, and salt. Cover with water and bring to a boil. Simmer for 1½ hours.

3. When the pork has been cooking for 30 minutes, prepare the sauerkraut. Take 2 cups of the pork cooking liquid and pour into another saucepan. Add the sauerkraut and bring to a boil.

4. Melt the drippings in the skillet and add the onions. Fry until golden brown, then add to the sauerkraut with the wine. Stir well and simmer for 40 minutes.

5. Stir the potato into the sauerkraut and simmer for a further 10 minutes. Add the sugar to take the edge off the sourness.

6. Arrange the pork and sauerkraut on a warmed serving platter and serve with mashed potatoes.

Serves 4

Himmel und Erde

(Potatoes with apple and sausage)

---

2 lb potatoes, peeled
2 lb apples, peeled, cored, and quartered
1 strip of lemon rind
4 teaspoons sugar
¼ lb slab bacon, diced
2 large onions, sliced
1 lb blood sausage, sliced

1. Cook the potatoes in boiling salted water until tender.

2. Meanwhile, cook the apples in another saucepan with the lemon rind and sugar until soft and pulpy. Discard the lemon rind.

3. Drain the potatoes and return to the pan. Dry out over a very gentle heat, then mash well. Beat in the apples until smooth. Keep hot.

4. Fry the bacon in a skillet until browned and crisp. Remove from the pan with a slotted spoon and stir into the potato mixture.

5. Add the onions to the skillet and fry in the bacon fat until golden brown. Stir into the potato mixture, with salt and pepper to taste.

6. Pile the potato mixture on a warmed serving plate and top with slices of blood sausage.

Serves 6–8

Loin of Pork
with Caraway Seed

6 tablespoons butter
2 tablespoons oil
1 × 3 lb boneless pork top loin roast
2 large onions, chopped
1 tablespoon paprika
1 cup dry white wine
⅔ cup chicken stock
2 tablespoons flour
1 cup sour cream
1 tablespoon chopped chives
1 tablespoon caraway seeds

1. Preheat the oven to 350°. Melt 4 tablespoons of the butter with the oil in a flameproof casserole. Add the pork and brown it on all sides. Remove the pork from the pot.

2. Add the onions to the casserole and fry until golden brown. Stir in the paprika, wine, and stock and bring to a boil. Return the pork to the casserole with salt and pepper to taste. Cover and transfer to the oven. Braise for about 1½ hours or until the pork is cooked through and tender.

3. Place the pork on a warmed serving platter and keep hot. Strain the cooking juices into a saucepan. Bring to a boil and boil until reduced by about one-quarter.

4. Mix the remaining butter with the flour to make a paste. Add a little of the cooking juices, then stir this mixture into the remaining juices in the pan. Simmer, stirring, until smooth and thickened. Stir in the sour cream, chives, and caraway seeds and heat gently. Serve this sauce with the pork.

Serves 4–6

31

Labskaus

(Corned beef hash)

---

2 tablespoons butter
2 large onions, finely chopped
1 lb canned corned beef, finely chopped
2 pickled herrings, drained and finely chopped
1 anchovy fillet, finely chopped
6 large potatoes, peeled, cooked, and mashed
1 teaspoon lemon juice

1. Melt the butter in a skillet. Add the onions and fry until softened. Stir in the remaining ingredients with pepper to taste and cook for 5 minutes, stirring occasionally.

2. Serve hot topped with poached or fried egg.

Serves 4

(Top) Loin of Pork with Caraway Seed
(Bottom) Labskaus

Kasseler Rippchen

(Smoked pork chops)

---

2 tablespoons butter
2 medium onions, chopped
2 medium carrots, peeled and sliced
2 large tomatoes, skinned, peeled, and chopped
6 large smoked pork chops
3 juniper berries, crushed
2 cups + 1 tablespoon cold water
2 teaspoons cornstarch
1 cup sour cream

1. Preheat the oven to 375°. Melt the butter in a flameproof casserole. Add the onions and carrots and fry until the onions are softened. Stir in the tomatoes and cook for a further 3 minutes.

2. Remove the casserole from the heat. Place the pork chops on top of the vegetables and sprinkle over the juniper berries. Add the 2 cups of water with salt and pepper to taste. Cover tightly and place in the oven. Cook for 30 minutes.

3. Reduce the oven temperature to 350° and uncover the casserole. Continue cooking for 40 minutes or until the chops are cooked through and browned. Transfer to a warmed serving platter, arranging the chops down the centre slightly overlapping. Keep hot.

4. Strain the cooking liquid into a saucepan, pressing down on the vegetables in the strainer with a wooden spoon. Bring to a boil. Dissolve the cornstarch in the remaining water and add to the pan. Simmer, stirring, until thickened. Stir in the sour cream, then pour this sauce over the chops.

Serves 6

Falscher Hase

(Mock hare)

½ lb beef chuck, cubed
1 lb boneless pork, cubed
2 juniper berries
1 teaspoon dried marjoram
2 thick slices of bread
milk
1 leek, chopped
2 onions, chopped
½ lb pork sausagemeat
4 eggs, beaten

1. Preheat the oven to 350°.

2. Mix the beef and pork with the juniper berries and marjoram. Moisten the bread with a little milk. Pass the meats, bread, leek, and onions twice through the grinder, or use a food processor. Add the sausagemeat, eggs, and salt to taste and mix together thoroughly.

3. Shape the mixture into a long roll with damp hands and place on a greased baking sheet. Alternatively, press the mixture into a loaf pan and place in a roasting pan containing hot water.

4. Bake for 1–1½ hours or until the loaf is golden brown.

Serves 4

German Country Supper

4 bacon slices, diced
1 medium onion, thinly sliced into rings
6 oz German sausage, such as fleischwurst, chopped
4 small potatoes, peeled, parboiled, and sliced
2 tablespoons butter
4 eggs
3 tablespoons grated cheese
chopped chives to garnish

1. Fry the bacon in a skillet until it is crisp and has rendered its fat. Add the onion, sausage, potatoes, and butter and cook, stirring, until the vegetables are lightly browned and the mixture is piping hot.

2. Beat the eggs lightly with the cheese and salt and pepper to taste. Pour over the mixture in the pan and stir to incorporate them with the sausage and vegetables. Cook gently until the eggs are lightly scrambled.

3. Serve hot, sprinkled with chives.

Serves 2–3

Venison with Pepper Sauce

4 venison chops
4 tablespoons oil
$\frac{3}{4}$ cup sour cream
1 teaspoon grated horseradish
Marinade
$\frac{1}{2}$ cup dry white wine
$\frac{1}{4}$ cup olive oil
1 onion, thinly sliced
1 garlic clove, crushed
12 black peppercorns
1 teaspoon dried thyme

1. Mix together the marinade ingredients in a shallow dish. Add the chops and turn to coat well. Leave to marinate in the refrigerator for 24 hours, turning occasionally. Drain the chops, reserving the marinade. Pat dry with paper towels.

2. Heat the oil in a frying pan. Add the chops and brown on both sides. Pour in the reserved marinade and bring to a boil. Cover and simmer for 20 minutes or until the chops are tender. Remove the pan from the heat and leave the chops to cool in the marinade. Cover and leave to marinate for a further 24 hours.

3. Return the pan to the heat and bring to a boil. Simmer for 15 minutes.

4. Transfer the chops to a warmed serving platter and keep hot. Strain the cooking marinade into a saucepan. Stir in the sour cream and horseradish and heat through gently. Pour this sauce over the chops and serve.

Serves 4

Hasenpfeffer

(Hare or rabbit casseroled in wine and herb sauce)

---

8 bacon slices
¾ cup flour
½ teaspoon dried thyme
1 × 5 lb hare (or rabbit), cleaned and cut into serving pieces
1 tablespoon butter
1 onion, finely chopped
2 garlic cloves, crushed
2 scallions, chopped
1 cup dry red wine
¾ cup chicken stock
1 tablespoon cranberry sauce
1 teaspoon chopped parsley
¼ teaspoon dried marjoram
grated rind of ½ lemon

1. Preheat the oven to 350°. Fry the bacon in a skillet until it is crisp. Remove the bacon from the skillet and drain on paper towels. Crumble and set aside. Mix the flour with the thyme and salt and pepper and use to coat the hare pieces.

2. Add the butter to the bacon fat in the skillet and heat it. Add the hare pieces, and brown on all sides, then transfer them to a casserole. Add the onion and garlic and fry until softened. Stir in the scallions and fry for 2 minutes. Transfer the vegetables to the casserole.

3. Pour all the fat from the skillet. Put in the wine and stock and bring to a boil, stirring. Stir in the cranberry sauce, herbs, and lemon rind. Pour over the hare and scatter over the bacon.

4. Cover the casserole and place it in the oven. Cook for 2½ hours or until the hare is very tender.

Serves 4–6

Roast Goose with Apple and Nut Stuffing

4 tablespoons butter
2 large onions, finely chopped
¾ lb pork sausagemeat
4 large tart apples, peeled, cored, and sliced
1 cup dried apricots, soaked overnight, drained, and chopped
grated rind of 2 oranges
1 cup toasted chopped filberts
2 cups fresh breadcrumbs
2 tablespoons chopped chives
½ teaspoon dried marjoram
1 × 8½ lb goose
1 lemon, quartered

1. Preheat the oven to 425°. Melt the butter in a large skillet. Add the onions and fry until softened. Add the sausagemeat and continue frying until it has lost its pinkness.

2. Remove the pan from the heat. Add the apples, apricots, orange rind, nuts, breadcrumbs, chives, marjoram, and salt and pepper to taste and mix together thoroughly.

3. Rub the goose inside and out with the lemon quarters. Discard the lemon. Prick the goose all over with a fork, especially around the thighs. Rub inside and out with salt and pepper. Fill with the stuffing, then truss.

4. Place the goose, breast up, on a rack in a roasting pan. Roast for 20 minutes, then reduce the oven temperature to 375°. Continue roasting for 2½ hours or until the goose is cooked: test by piercing the thigh with a skewer – the juices that run out should be clear.

Serves 6

SALADS &
VEGETABLES

Kartoffelsalat

(Potato salad)

---

1 lb potatoes, peeled and quartered
6 bacon slices
1 small onion, finely chopped
2 tablespoons wine vinegar or lemon juice
¼ teaspoon dry mustard
1 teaspoon caraway seeds

1. Cook the potatoes in boiling salted water until tender.

2. Meanwhile, fry the bacon in a skillet until it is crisp and has rendered its fat. Drain the bacon on paper towels and crumble.

3. Add the onion to the bacon fat and fry until softened. Remove the onion from the skillet with a slotted spoon and set aside.

4. Add the vinegar or lemon juice, mustard, caraway seeds, and salt and pepper to taste to the skillet and mix well. Remove from the heat and keep hot.

5. Drain the potatoes and cut them into cubes. Put into a large salad bowl and add the crumbled bacon and onion. Pour over the hot dressing and toss together thoroughly. Serve hot or cold.

Serves 4

Kopfsalat mit Buttermilch

(Lettuce salad with buttermilk dressing)

---

1 head of Boston lettuce, shredded
2 small potatoes, peeled, cooked, and diced
4 bacon slices, fried until crisp and crumbled
4 small dill pickles, finely chopped
1 small onion, thinly sliced into rings
Dressing
$\frac{3}{4}$ cup buttermilk
1 teaspoon brown sugar
1 teaspoon lemon juice

1. Put the lettuce, potatoes, bacon, pickles, and onion in a salad bowl.

2. Put all the dressing ingredients in a screwtop jar and shake until well combined.

3. Pour the dressing over the salad and toss well. Serve immediately.

Serves 4

(Previous page)
(Top) Roast Goose with Apple and Nut Stuffing
(Bottom) Kartoffelsalat

43

Zwiebelkuchen

(Onion tart)

$1\frac{1}{2}$ cups flour
3 tablespoons butter
3 tablespoons lard
4–5 tablespoons iced water
Filling
2 tablespoons butter
3 medium onions, thinly sliced
2 eggs, beaten
$\frac{3}{4}$ cup light cream
1 teaspoon caraway seeds

1. Preheat the oven to 400°. Sift the flour and a pinch of salt into a mixing bowl. Rub in the butter and lard until the mixture resembles breadcrumbs, then bind to a dough with the iced water.

2. Roll out the dough on a lightly floured surface and use to line a 9-inch tart or pie pan. Prick all over with a fork, then line with foil and half fill with dried beans or rice. Bake the case for 10 minutes. Remove the foil and beans or rice and continue baking for 5 minutes or until set and golden brown. Remove from the oven and set aside. Reduce the temperature to 375°.

3. For the filling, melt the butter in a skillet. Add the onions and fry until softened. Remove from the heat.

4. Lightly beat the eggs with the cream, caraway seeds, and salt and pepper to taste. Stir in the onions. Pour the filling into the pastry case.

5. Bake the tart for 40 minutes or until the filling is risen and golden brown. Serve hot or cold.

Serves 4–6

Leipziger Allerlei

(Mixed vegetables in cream sauce)

---

1 small head of cauliflower, broken into florets
1 cup shelled peas
½ lb asparagus spears, cut into 1 inch pieces
1½ cups green beans
4 small carrots, peeled and diced
4 small button mushrooms
Sauce
2 tablespoons butter
2 tablespoons flour
1 cup milk
1 cup cream
1 teaspoon dried chervil
1 teaspoon lemon juice

1. Cook the cauliflower and peas in simmering water for about 10 minutes. Add the asparagus, beans, and carrots and cook for a further 5 minutes. Add the mushrooms and cook for a final 5 minutes or until all the vegetables are just tender.

2. Meanwhile, for the sauce, melt the butter in a saucepan. Stir in the flour and cook for 1 minute. Gradually stir in the milk and cream and bring to a boil, stirring. Simmer until thickened. Stir in the chervil, lemon juice, and salt and pepper to taste.

3. Drain the vegetables and put into a warmed serving bowl. Pour over the sauce and fold gently together. Serve hot.

Serves 4

DESSERTS & CAKES

Apfelbettelmann

(Apple pudding)

½ cup raisins
6 tablespoons orange juice
grated rind of 1 small lemon
4 cups fresh breadcrumbs, made from pumpernickel bread
1 cup brown sugar
1 cup chopped almonds
1 teaspoon ground allspice
7 tablespoons butter, melted
1½ lb tart apples, peeled, cored, and thinly sliced

1. Mix together the raisins, orange juice and lemon rind in a mixing bowl and leave to soak for 30 minutes. Preheat the oven to 350°.

2. Add the breadcrumbs, sugar, almonds, spice, and 4 tablespoons of the butter to the raisin mixture and combine well. Put about one-third of the breadcrumb mixture on the bottom of a buttered 1½ quart capacity baking dish and cover with half the apple slices. Add another third of the breadcrumb mixture followed by the rest of the apples. Cover with the remaining breadcrumb mixture. Pour the remaining melted butter over the top.

3. Bake for 35 minutes and serve hot.

Serves 6

Berliner Pfannkuchen

(Plum doughnuts)

1½ packages active dry yeast
1½ cups lukewarm milk
½ cup sugar
6 cups flour
2 eggs
1 egg yolk
grated rind of 1 lemon
few drops of vanilla extract
4 tablespoons butter, melted
¾ cup plum jam
oil for deep frying
sugar for sprinkling

1. Stir the yeast into a little of the milk and add 2 teaspoons of the sugar. Leave in a warm place for about 20 minutes or until frothy.

2. Sift the flour and remaining sugar into a mixing bowl. Add the eggs and egg yolk, lemon rind, a pinch of salt, vanilla, melted butter, remaining milk, and the yeast mixture. Beat to a dough.

3. Place the dough on a floured surface and roll out to the thickness of a finger. Cut into 3 inch rounds. Put a little jam in the center of half of the dough rounds and put the remaining rounds on top. Press the edges together to seal, with damp fingers.

4. Leave the doughnuts in a warm place to rise for 10 minutes.

5. Deep fry the doughnuts, in batches, until they are golden brown all over. Drain on paper towels and sprinkle with sugar while they are still warm.

Makes about 16

Schwarzbrotpudding

(Black bread pudding)

$\frac{1}{2}$ lb cranberries
1 teaspoon lemon juice
3 eggs, separated
1 cup sugar
1 vanilla bean
$\frac{1}{2}$ teaspoon ground cinnamon
4 cups breadcrumbs, made from black bread
3 oz (3 squares) semisweet chocolate, grated
whipped cream to decorate

1. Preheat the oven to 350°. Put the cranberries in a saucepan with the lemon juice and just enough water to cover the bottom of the pan. Stew gently until the cranberries are tender.

2. Meanwhile, beat the egg yolks, sugar, vanilla from the bean, and cinnamon together until pale and thick. Fold in the breadcrumbs. Beat the egg whites until stiff and fold into the breadcrumb mixture.

3. Drain the cranberries. Spread half of them over the bottom of a buttered $1\frac{1}{2}$ quart baking dish. Cover with half the breadcrumb mixture and scatter over all the chocolate. Add the rest of the cranberries and finally the remaining breadcrumb mixture.

4. Cover the dish with foil and bake for 50 minutes. Cool the pudding, then decorate with whipped cream.

Serves 8

Frankfurter Kranz

(*Buttercream layer cake*)

$2\frac{1}{2}$ cups flour
2 teaspoons baking powder
$\frac{1}{2}$ lb (2 sticks) butter
1 cup sugar
6 eggs, separated
1 teaspoon finely grated lemon rind
3 tablespoons rum
Buttercream
12 tablespoons ($1\frac{1}{2}$ sticks) unsalted butter
6 cups confectioners' sugar, sifted
1 tablespoon vanilla extract
4 tablespoons whipping cream

1. Preheat the oven to 300°. Sift the flour and baking powder into a bowl. In another bowl, cream the butter with the sugar until light and fluffy. Beat the egg yolks into the creamed mixture, one at a time. Fold in the flour mixture and the lemon rind.

2. Beat the egg whites until stiff and fold into the batter. Spoon into a buttered and floured 9 inch tube pan. Bake for $1-1\frac{1}{4}$ hours or until a skewer inserted into the center of the cake comes out clean.

3. Meanwhile, make the buttercream. Cream the butter until soft, then gradually beat in the sugar and a pinch of salt. When the mixture is pale and fluffy, beat in the vanilla and cream.

4. Cool the cake on a rack, then slice into three layers. Sprinkle each layer with rum and sandwich back together with about half the buttercream. Spread the remaining buttercream over the top and sides of the assembled cake.

Serves 8

Schwarzwaldkuchen

(Black Forest cherry cake)

---

5 eggs
$\frac{3}{4}$ cup sugar
$\frac{1}{2}$ cup flour
$\frac{1}{2}$ cup unsweetened cocoa powder
10 tablespoons butter, melted
Syrup
$\frac{1}{2}$ cup sugar
1 cup water
Filling
4 cups whipping cream
$\frac{1}{2}$ cup confectioners' sugar
$\frac{1}{2}$ lb canned Morello or Bing cherries, drained and dried
chocolate curls to decorate

1. Preheat the oven to 350°. Beat the eggs and sugar until fluffy. Sift over the flour and cocoa and fold in with the butter. Divide between 3 buttered 7 inch layer cake pans. Bake for 12–15 minutes or until a skewer inserted into the center of each cake comes out clean. Cool in the pan for 10 minutes, then cool completely on a rack.

2. To make the syrup, dissolve the sugar in the water. Boil for 5 minutes. Cool for 20 minutes, then prick the surfaces of the cakes and soak in the syrup.

3. Whip the cream with the sugar until thick. Spread a layer of cream over one of the cakes and cover with the cherries. Place another cake on top and spread with cream. Put the third cake on top. Spread about two-thirds of the remaining cream over the sides. Decorate with chocolate curls. Pipe the remaining cream onto the top of the cake and decorate with maraschino cherries and more chocolate curls.

Serves 10

Apfelstrudel

$2\frac{1}{2}$ cups flour
1 egg, beaten
1 cup lukewarm water
2 tablespoons butter, melted
Filling
3 lb sweet apples, peeled, cored, and thinly sliced
1 cup raisins
$\frac{3}{4}$ cup chopped almonds or walnuts
8 tablespoons (1 stick) butter, melted
1 cup fresh breadcrumbs

1. Sift the flour and a pinch of salt into a bowl. Mix together the egg, water and melted butter and add to the flour. Mix to a firm dough. Place on a floured surface and knead until it is smooth and elastic. Cover and leave for 30 minutes.

2. Meanwhile, make the filling. Mix together the apples, raisins, and nuts.

3. Spread out a large cloth on a table and sprinkle with flour. Place the dough on the cloth and roll out as thinly as possible. Lift and stretch the dough, pulling it until it is paper thin. Trim the edges so the sides are straight.

4. Preheat the oven to 450°. Brush the dough with half the melted butter and sprinkle with almost all of the crumbs. Spoon the apple mixture in a long strip onto the dough. Lift the dough over the filling and roll it up. Tuck in the ends. Brush with the remaining butter and sprinkle over the rest of the crumbs.

5. Cut the roll into pieces to fit onto greased baking sheets. Place the pieces on the sheets, seam underneath. Bake for 10 minutes, then reduce the oven temperature to 400°. Continue baking for 20 minutes or until crisp and golden.

Serves 24

Dampfnudeln

(Sweet dumplings)

$\frac{1}{2}$ package active dry yeast
3 tablespoons lukewarm water
2 tablespoons sugar
$2\frac{1}{2}$ cups flour
$\frac{1}{4}$ teaspoon salt
$\frac{1}{2}$ cup lukewarm milk
2 tablespoons butter, melted
Cooking liquid
2 tablespoons butter
2 tablespoons sugar
$\frac{1}{2}$ cup milk

1. Stir the yeast into the water and add $\frac{1}{2}$ teaspoon of the sugar. Leave in a warm place for about 20 minutes or until frothy.

2. Sift the flour, salt, and remaining sugar into a bowl. Add the milk, melted butter, and yeast mixture and beat to a smooth dough. Knead the dough for about 5 minutes or until elastic. Leave in a warm place to rise for 1 hour or until doubled in bulk.

3. Punch down the dough, then divide it into 12 pieces. Shape into balls. Place the balls on a baking sheet and leave in a warm place to rise for 45 minutes to 1 hour.

4. To prepare the cooking liquid, melt the butter in a wide, shallow saucepan and stir in the sugar and milk. Bring to a boil. Place the dumplings in the pan, side by side, cover tightly and simmer gently for 20 minutes or until the dumplings are tender and have absorbed all the liquid. Serve hot, with stewed fruit.

Serves 4–6

Mandeltorte

(Almond layer cake)

---

1 cup fresh breadcrumbs
6 tablespoons milk
2 tablespoons brandy
4 tablespoons butter
6 tablespoons sugar
6 eggs, separated
1 cup ground almonds
Filling
1¼ cups whipping cream
1 tablespoon brandy
¼ cup confectioners' sugar
½ cup slivered almonds

1. Preheat the oven to 350°. Put the breadcrumbs in a bowl and sprinkle over the milk and brandy. Leave to soak.

2. Cream the butter with the sugar until light and fluffy. Beat in the egg yolks, one at a time. Add the breadcrumb mixture and almonds and mix well.

3. Beat the egg whites until stiff and fold into the almond mixture. Divide the batter between two buttered 8 inch layer cake pans.

4. Bake for 40 minutes or until the cakes spring back when lightly pressed in the center. Cool on a rack.

5. To make the filling, whip the cream with the brandy and sugar until thick. Use to sandwich together the cake layers and sprinkle the almonds on the top.

Serves 10

Lebkuchen

(Spice cake)

---

3 eggs
$\frac{3}{4}$ cup sugar
$1\frac{1}{4}$ cups clear honey
1 cup finely chopped almonds
grated rind of $\frac{1}{2}$ lemon
grated rind of $\frac{1}{2}$ orange
$\frac{1}{3}$ cup chopped mixed candied peel
$2\frac{1}{2}$ cups flour
1 teaspoon baking powder
$\frac{1}{4}$ teaspoon ground cloves
$\frac{1}{2}$ teaspoon ground cinnamon
$\frac{1}{8}$ teaspoon grated nutmeg

1. Preheat the oven to 375°. Beat the eggs and sugar together until pale and fluffy. Stir in the honey, almonds, lemon and orange rind, and candied peel. Sift together the flour, baking powder and spices and fold into the honey mixture.

2. Pour into a greased 8 inch square cake pan. Bake for 40–45 minutes or until a skewer inserted into the center of the cake comes out clean.

3. Cool on a rack.

Serves 16

Käsekuchen

(Cheesecake)

1½ cups crushed graham crackers
6 tablespoons butter, melted
½ cup sugar
1 teaspoon ground cinnamon
2 eggs, beaten
¼ teaspoon salt
grated rind and juice of ½ lemon
½ cup light cream
1 cup cottage cheese
½ cup chopped mixed nuts

1. Preheat the oven to 350°. Mix together the graham cracker crumbs, melted butter, 2 tablespoons of the sugar and the cinnamon. Reserve 2 tablespoons of this mixture, then press the remainder over the bottom and sides of a greased 8 inch layer cake pan. Chill until set.

2. Beat the eggs with the salt, lemon rind and juice, cream, cottage cheese, and remaining sugar. Fold in half the nuts. Pour the cheese mixture into the crumb crust and sprinkle the remaining nuts and the reserved crumb mixture on top.

3. Bake for 35–45 minutes or until a skewer inserted into the center of the cake comes out clean.

4. Turn off the oven, open the door and leave the cheesecake inside to cool for 10 minutes. Remove from the oven and cool to room temperature.

Serves 8

Bremerkuchen

(Bremen sweetbread)

---

2 packages active dry yeast
½ cup lukewarm water
½ cup sugar
3¼ cups milk
10 tablespoons butter
12 cups flour
1 teaspoon salt
½ teaspoon ground cardamom
grated rind of 3 lemons
1½ cups raisins
1 cup slivered almonds

1. Stir the yeast into the water with ½ teaspoon of the sugar. Leave in a warm place for about 20 minutes or until frothy. Scald the milk. Add 8 tablespoons of the butter and heat until it has melted. Remove from the heat and cool to lukewarm.

2. Sift the flour, remaining sugar, salt and cardamom into a bowl. Add the yeast and milk mixtures and the lemon rind, and mix to a dough. Knead for about 10 minutes or until smooth and elastic. Leave in a warm place to rise until doubled in bulk.

3. Punch down the dough. Add the raisins, and half the almonds and work into the dough until they are evenly distributed. Cut into two pieces and shape into long loaves. Place on greased baking sheets. Cover and rise for 45 minutes.

4. Preheat the oven to 375°. Press the remaining almonds into the tops of the loaves. Bake for 1 hour. Melt the remaining butter. Remove the loaves from the oven and brush the tops with the melted butter. Serve cool.

Makes 2 loaves

Stollen

(Christmas sweet bread)

---

1 package active dry yeast
$\frac{3}{4}$ cup sugar
$\frac{3}{4}$ cup milk
8 tablespoons (1 stick) butter
4 cups flour
1 teaspoon salt
$\frac{1}{2}$ teaspoon ground cinnamon
2 eggs, beaten
1 cup chopped mixed candied peel
$\frac{1}{2}$ cup seedless white raisins
$\frac{1}{2}$ cup chopped walnuts
Frosting
2 tablespoons butter, melted
2 cups confectioners' sugar, sifted
2 tablespoons water

1. Stir the yeast into a little lukewarm water and $\frac{1}{2}$ teaspoon of the sugar. Leave in a warm place for 20 minutes or until frothy. Scald the milk. Add the butter and heat until melted. Remove from the heat and cool to lukewarm.

2. Sift the flour, remaining sugar, salt, and spice into a bowl. Add the yeast and milk mixtures and the eggs and mix to a dough. Knead until smooth and elastic. Leave until doubled in bulk.

3. Punch down the dough. Add the peel, raisins and nuts and work into the dough until evenly distributed. Shape into an oval and place on a greased baking sheet. Leave for 45 minutes.

4. Preheat the oven to 400°. Bake for 15 minutes, then reduce the oven to 350°. Continue baking for 30 minutes.

5. To make the frosting, beat together all the ingredients until smooth. Spread over the top of the stollen.

Spritzgebäck

(Filbert cookies)

$\frac{1}{2}$ *lb (2 sticks) butter*
1 cup sugar
1 egg, beaten
1 teaspoon vanilla extract
$\frac{1}{4}$ *teaspoon grated nutmeg*
$2\frac{1}{2}$ *cups flour*
$\frac{1}{2}$ *teaspoon baking powder*
$\frac{1}{2}$ *cup ground filberts*
1 tablespoon confectioners' sugar

1. Preheat the oven to 350°. Cream the butter with the sugar until light and fluffy. Beat in the egg, vanilla, and nutmeg. Sift the flour with the baking powder, then fold into the creamed mixture with the nuts.

2. Spoon the mixture into a piping bag fitted with a $\frac{1}{2}$ inch plain nozzle. Pipe the mixture in spirals onto baking sheets.

3. Bake for 10–15 minutes or until the cookies are just firm to the touch and golden brown around the edges.

4. Cool on the baking sheets for 5 minutes, then cool completely on a rack. Sift the confectioners' sugar over the cookies before serving.

Makes about 40

INDEX